This book is proudly dedicated to all the kids and wildlife lovers that prowl upon this BEAUTIFUL PLANET.

💜💜🧡🧡

Walking Stick  **Goalie Mask**  **Camera**  **Golf Ball**

Ring  **Surfboard**  **Owl Toque**  **Necklace**

Dream Catcher  **USB Stick** 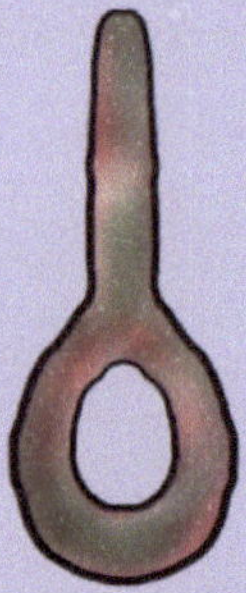 **Sour Key**  Jay's Canada Book

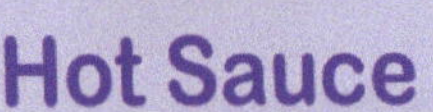

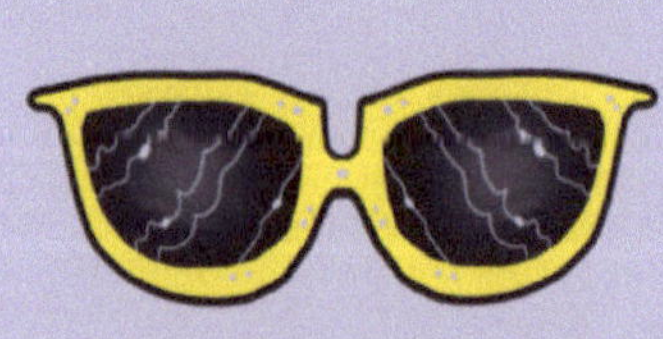

Hot Sauce **Hat** **Sunglasses**

WRITTEN BY/PHOTOGRAPHY BY: JASON GEORGE

ILLUSTRATED BY: JIMMY MCGANN

TABLE OF CONTENTS

@jasongeorgephotography
@jimmy_mcgann_art

There are over 160 different primates on the continent of Africa. They not only have the smallest primate, but also the largest of primates on earth. How many primates have you seen?

Baboons, Colobus Monkeys, Drills, Geladas, Guenons, Mandrills, One Macaque Species, Mangabeys, Patas Monkeys, Vervet Monkeys

One day I was driving to the Cape of Good Hope with my parents to see where the Atlantic Ocean meets the Indian Ocean. We noticed a small troop of about a hundred Baboons just hanging out by the side of the road. Baboon troops can get up to over three hundred individuals!

Vervet Monkey

I wish I could drive

One morning as I left my tent for a stroll, I heard a loud thud. As I looked around I saw a young Baboon with what seemed to be an injured leg. I guess even Monkeys can miss branches. The small Baboon was fine in the end and hopped along his way shortly after.

Ostriches are the largest bird I've ever seen in the wild and their eggs can be a bit bigger than a 500ml tub of delicious ice cream. Although Ostriches are large, they can hit speeds up to 70km an hour! ...That's just a little bit faster than me.

Male Ostriches are much darker than females

Like chickens, the female Ostrich is called a hen and the male is a rooster

Flocks of Ostriches can reach up to a hundred birds, but most only have about ten in them. A hundred would be scary!

Common Ostrich
Somali Ostrich

Mental health day at the watering hole

The fish I caught was this big!

The Great White Pelican likes to hang around alkaline lakes…

…but can be found by coastal estuarine areas…

…as they like the mixture of fresh and salt water.

I don't know if Zebras are black with white stripes, or white with black stripes...
...I just know that they are beautiful and that each Zebra has it's own unique pattern.
Zebras are single hoofed animals and are closely related to Horses.

I can see you lion.
A Zebra should stand out in the wild against the greens and browns, but it doesn't because their predators only see in black and white.
I smell Zebra...
Mountain Zebra
Grévy's Zebra
Plains Zebra

The most interesting fact that
I learned about Hyenas while I
was in Africa was that they are
able to digest the bones, horns
and teeth of their prey.

Spotted Hyena
Striped Hyena
Brown Hyena

Hyenas are Africa's most common large carnivore.
They often hunt alone, unless the prey is too large.

Hyenas actually help balance food resources by weeding out the weak and sicker hoofed animals.
Spotted Hyenas have a strict alpha female social structure.

FUN FACT: Only male Dik-Dik's have horns.

I didn't even know that the Dik-Dik existed before I went to Africa and that's why it might be my favourite animal of the entire trip. I'd say the Dik-Dik looks like a baby deer, jumps around like a bunny and is about the size of a house cat. Unlike most African antelopes the Dik-Dik does not live in a herd, but instead create a monogamous pairing and protect their own territory.

Günther's Dik-Dik, Kirk's Dik-Dik, Silver Dik-Dik, Salt's Dik-Dik

Both male and female Giraffes can grow to heights of 16 feet! But unfortunately most of them die at a young age, falling to lions, hyenas, leopards, crocs, insects and parasites. When threatened Giraffes will not only use their hooves for fighting, but they will swing their heads at an enemy. Surprisingly, Giraffes can run at speeds up to 35mph!
Beautiful!

The funniest thing to me about a Giraffe is their tongues, cause they feel like rough, rough sand paper. Once a Giraffe wrapped it's tongue around my hand and I kinda jumped cause the feeling was soooo strange. It felt just like giant cat tongue.

Masai Giraffe, Northern Giraffe, Southern Giraffe, Reticulated Giraffe

One night in Africa while I was fast asleep some Hippos came into our camp and started grazing beside our tents. They soon had enough to eat and returned to the water. When food is scarce Hippopotamuses can go up to 3 weeks without eating, because they are able to survive on the food stored up in their stomach's.

Translated in Greek, the word Hippopotamus means "water horse", or "river horse."
But Hippos don't actually swim, they kind of just glide along and push themselves off of objects on the bottom of the water.

I was walking along to see and photograph more Hippos when suddenly I tripped and fell. When I looked back to see what I had tripped over I saw it was a Hippopotamus tooth! It was huge and sharp. No wonder they are considered the most deadly large land mammal in Africa.

There is only one species of Lion - Panthera Leo.
Female Lionesses are attracted to the males that have the longest and darkest manes. However, these thick manes can also lead to overheating. Lions are the most social cats, with prides up to 30 members.
JGP
GEORGE

I was told that Lions normally drink before they feed and to my surprise I saw a few cubs come down to the water before they ran off to eat their dinner.

FUN FACTS: A Lion's roar can be heard 8km away!

Both male and female Penguins take care of the baby chicks. While one goes out to catch squid and fish, the other mate will stay with the eggs, or chicks to protect them from predators.

I had more than a couple African Penguins bump and waddle into me as I took photos and I was so surprised when I heard that they sound exactly like donkeys. Hee-haw!!

I was so excited to head out to the Cape of Good Hope with my parents as we were going to see the Penguins. Did you know that Penguins don't just live in the snow?

African Penguin

Rhinoceroses have poor eyesight, but their acute sense of smell and hearing make up for this. Although the White Rhino is larger than the Black Rhino, it is difficult to tell them apart as they are both grey in colour.

The White Rhino can run up to 40km per hour, while the Black Rhino can get up to 55km per hour for short distances.

Rhinoceroses have a symbiotic relationship with a bird called the Oxpecker. These birds help remove ticks and clear any pesky parasites from any open wound.

I was able to see both types of Rhino while I was in Africa, however I only saw one White Rhino briefly before it ran into the bushes. A very special moment for me as this species is nearly extinct.

I was in a hot air balloon over 2000 feet in the air when we SPOTTED a leopard on the ground. We dropped down for a few photos before it vanished into the bush.

I've SPOTTED a Leopard!!!!!
Leopards are generally solitary animals that like to hang out in dense bushes, or high up in a sturdy tree. They are mostly nocturnal, so seeing one is rare as they are also timid masters of camouflage.
African Leopard- Pardus Pardus
Leopards have beautiful rose-like markings referred to as rosettes.

In Canada we usually swerve our cars for squirrels and raccoons, but imagine having to swerve for an animal that is the size of a garbage truck. Elephants can weigh up to 6 tons! That's like 54.5 Jason's.

Savanna Elephant
Forest Elephant

The tusks of an elephant are actually extended upper incisor teeth and both male and female elephants have them. In between those two large tusks is the elephant's trunk, which is used for many different things such as: vocalizing, greeting, feeding, drinking, bathing and many other social behaviours.

Elephants live in large matriarchal social herds and they graze and wander in over 35 African countries.

Cheetahs are often confused with leopards, but cheetahs have solid spots, not rosettes and instead of roaring, they chirp. Cheetahs tend to do most of their hunting in the day as there are fewer predators around that could potentially steal their kills. I plan on returning to Africa one day soon so I can see more of these beautiful creatures.

Cheetahs are the fastest land animal and can run up to 102km/h! As a child they were my favourite animal and I was lucky enough to seen them on my trip to Africa.

Great white sharks have muscular torpedo shaped bodies that allow them to pick up speed quickly in the water. They have 300 teeth in their mouths. Luckily I was not on the meal menu.

I was walking down the street one day in Africa when I saw a sign about sharks. I investigated and was able to set up a trip to a place called Shark Alley. This is where sharks gather to feed on seals, who are rich in protein.

When we got to our location we got inside of cages and were lowered into the water. I saw 8 sharks right up close and some were up to 20 feet long. The scariest moment was when a shark bumped right into the cage I was in!

MEET JASON'S ADOPTION CREW!

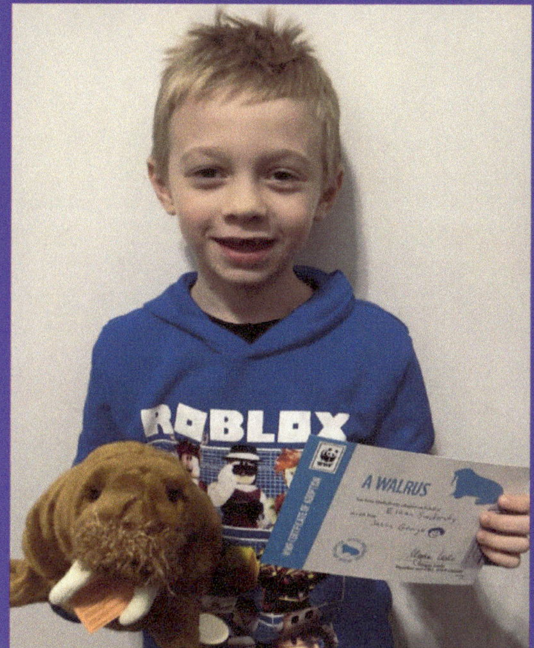

Auditions for the next book are open now!!

THE JGP PROWL

The JGP Prowl is a wildlife club that Jason George created in 2022 to bring wildlife lovers together to tell fun stories and connect with others through events that he plans and hosts.

The JGP Prowl membership will give access and deals to multiple items created by Jason now and in the future. This membership includes:

1 limited edition safari hat (which Jason helped sew)
1 membership card
1 photo card
1 mailed birthday card
4 meetings a year (2 virtual - Feb 12th, July 2nd and 2 in person - May 28, Oct 1st
1 free kids entry to the Wye Marsh
4 newsletters (1 per season. Event info, updates and games)
VIP access to books (even before his family!)
15% off birthday parties, tours, 2024 membership
Prizes at every meeting for those in attendance (crystals, prints and more!)
If you attend all 4 you will receive a high quality acrylic print, plus a chance to win a 2024 pass!

JGP

JGP PROWL

JGP PROWL

Wyatt

French Woods

JAY'S CHALLENGES!!

CHALLENGE #1

This challenge will help you to sharpen your observation skills in your day-to-day life. Here's how it works:

1. THE COLOUR PURPLE
2. OBJECTS (see Jason's item list)
3. ANIMALS (any animal in this book)

If you see the colour purple give yourself 1 point. If you see a purple item (for example: a purple camera) then give yourself 2 points. (1 purple + 1 item = 2) Now if you see a purple camera in the hands of a squirrel give yourself 3 points! (1 purple + 1 item + 1 animal = 3 points) Keep track of your scores, have fun and see how many things you can spot!

CHALLENGE #2

This is a photography challenge. I want you to take a photo of new flora, or fauna. Flora is any kind of plant life you may find interesting enough to photograph. Fauna is any kind of animal you can manage to snap an interesting shot of. Submit photos to jasongeorgephotography@gmail.com and a few select images will be in the next book! Have fun and always try and spread good deeds :)

Hi,

Thank you for taking the time to read the second book in this series "The World With Jason George." There are more to come! I hope that you enjoyed Jimmy's illustrations as much as I did and the new colouring feature is so much fun.

Being a dyslexic BIPOC wildlife photographer, presenter and writer is tough at times, but so much fun at other times. I was recently working on book 3 and had the privilege of helping some critically endangered hawksbill turtles. We were able to witness a mother lay hundreds of eggs, we helped move 546 eggs and saw 812 babies crawl out to sea. I even swam with a few of them! Don't worry I shared the experience on my YouTube channel. Go check it out! Make sure you subscribe and don't miss out.

Until next time, stay safe and keep enjoying wildlife.

Jason George

Can you guess where Jason will go to next? Here's a hint >

Hello,

First off I'd like to thank all the wildlife lovers out there that have taken the time to read these books. Illustrating has always been a dream of mine and I couldn't be having more fun doing these books.

I'd also like to thank Jason George for his love and passion for these projects and for the respect and admiration he has for all animals and his impressive photography.

Stay tuned, because we have so much more in the works!

Thanks again,

Jimmy McGann

SEE IF YOU CAN GUESS THE ANIMAL'S FOOTPRINTS!

ANSWERS: 1. LION 2. GIRAFFE 3. MONKEY 4. HYENA 5. PELICAN 6. LEOPARD 7. ZEBRA 8. PENGUIN 9. SHARK 10. JASON 11. ELEPHANT 12. DIK-DIK

Jason George
JG
Photography

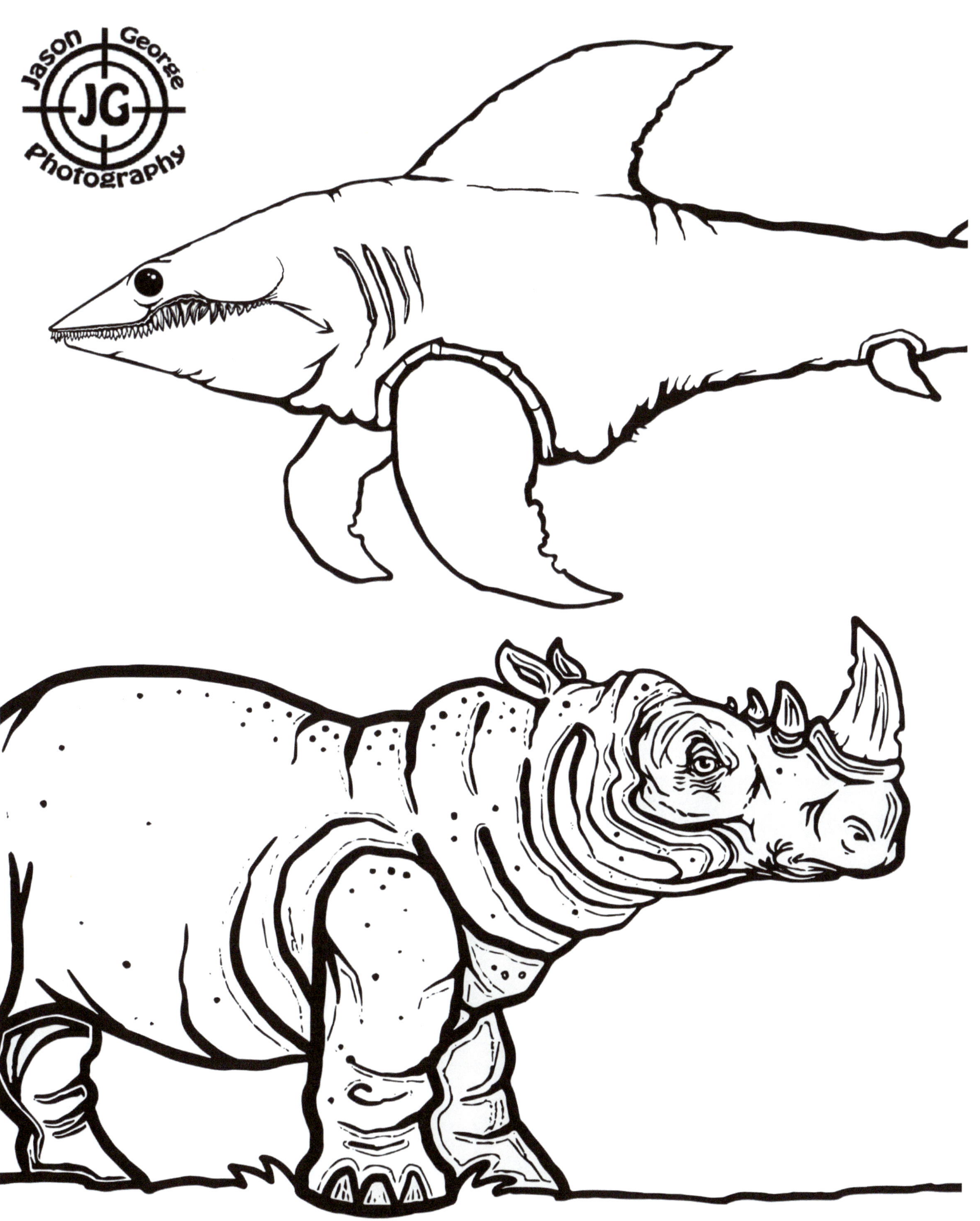

Photocopy these pages and add your own colours!

Use these QR code's to see Jason's wild and exciting videos and photos. Videos such as: a baby sea turtle's first breath of salt air, a loon hatching, a melanistic red fox, baby barred owls and so much more!

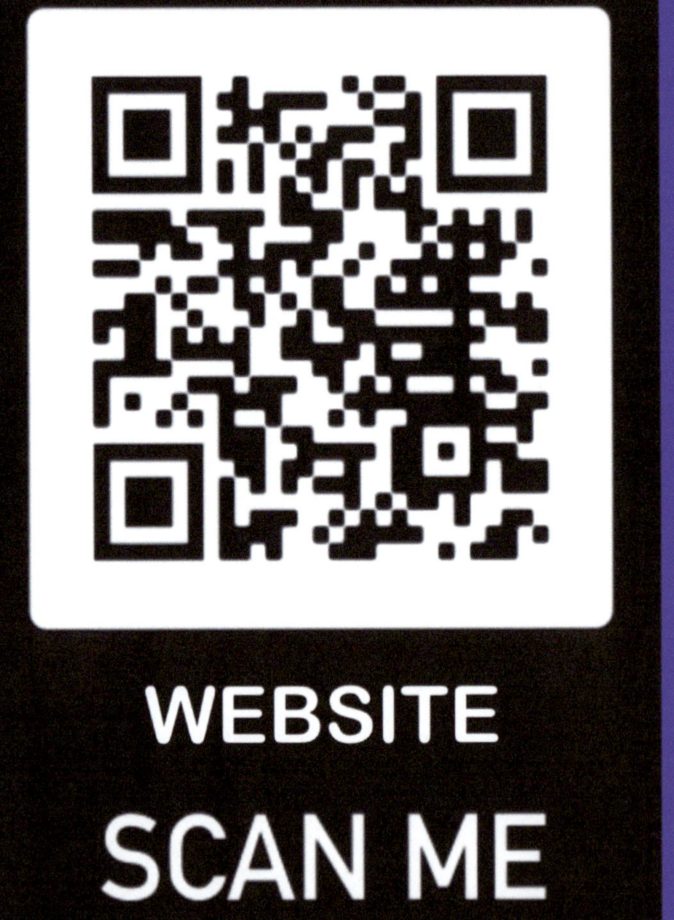

Jason is working on a series "Going Deeper" where he will share some never before seen footage and explain more about specific animals such as: owls, foxes, beavers and so much more!

Where in the
World should we
go next??